THE RAILW... STRATHM...
(PERTH, FORFAR AND BRECHIN)

By
C. T. GOODE

1988
ISBN 1 870313 05 4
72 Woodland Drive, Anlaby, Hull. HU10 7HX.

Contents

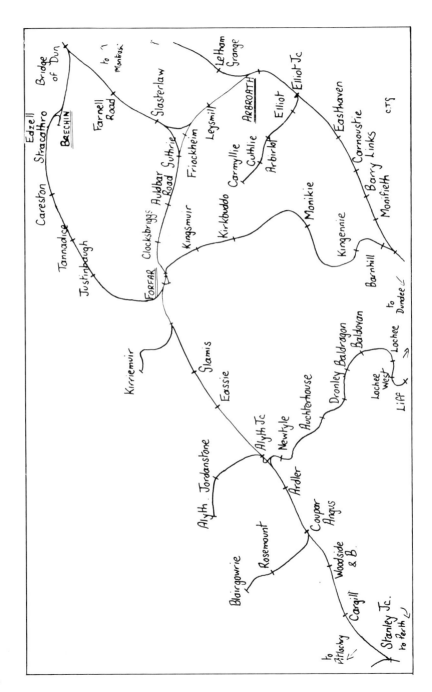

Foreword

Strathmore is a little out of my usual orbit, but I was encouraged to do something on the railways in that pleasant part of the world after a holiday spent there last year, when the first thing that struck me was how so much railway activity could vanish for ever, leaving almost nothing of what must have been a bustling scene at one time. I hope that this little book and Mr. Robin's evocative pictures will bring some of it back to life again. I am indeed grateful for his kind assistance and also for that given by Ed. Nicoll.

C. Tony Goode.

Anlaby, Hull. 1988.

Designed & Printed by
Swannack Brown & Co. Ltd.,
13a Anlaby Road, Hull.

The Railways of Strathmore

Chapter 1

The Vale of Strathmore lies quietly to the north of Dundee and the Tay estuary, over the Sidlaw hills which form an effective barrier rising in places to 1,500ft. Then, again, north of Strathmore lie the Grampians, a different proposition of wilder and grander aspect. Within the confines of this broad, flat valley the soil is fertile and settlements are fairly few and not too large; Forfar, Blairgowrie and Coupar Angus make perhaps the greatest impression. The logical current of commerce would be either east or westwards, the former if one sought the coast at Aberbeen, and the original roads were laid down in an easy pattern in those directions.

It would be sensible, therefore, to plan the development of railways along similar lines; however, this was not so and there was a strong movement within the powers of Dundee to tap the resources of the hinterland which lay so near and yet so far. Dundee had grown up on its jute, flax and hemp industries and had a flourishing seaborne trade; however, being somewhat trapped along its coastline and continuing to expand, it saw the benefits of supplies of building stone and slates, soil for the growth of produce and fresh water, and saw also the imminent danger of all these passing off regularly to Arbroath and Montrose in due course.

At first tentative suggestions were made for the provision of a canal over the Sidlaw barrier, as mentioned in early newspaper articles of 1817, though this idea, popular generally as a means of transport, failed to gain support here; instead the town council of Dundee arranged consultations with wealthy land-owners likely to be involved in the building of a railway line from Dundee into Strathmore. The idea was floated in January 1825 and £100 was earmarked towards the cost of surveying the line of route. Subscribers were canvassed and, on 1st. February 1825 a meeting was called and Charles Landale was given the task of surveying a suitable route. Of three possible routes he chose the one which, in hindsight, was the least likely to succeed and which, at this early stage in the history of railway development generally, favoured stationary engines and inclines rather than wheeled traction of the self-propelled kind. Thus, the line of way had three inclines and two levels, facts which might have been, though each end of the line was incomplete,with the Dundee end falling short of the essential docks and the north end landing in a field near Newtyle mill. An Act for the construction of the line was passed on 26th. May 1826 and various tenders were sought.

Excluding purchase of the land, the total cost of the line was £25,600, of which £18,000 comprised eleven miles of track with fish-bellied rails in cast-iron chairs on stone sleepers, set to a gauge of 4 ft. 6½ in. Out of Dundee the line immediately went through a short tunnel north of the town-in these days it was often de rigueur to have such a feature to please the customers-a fact which caused problems as excavation revealed rubble instead of rock, necessitating the expense of lining. Three stationary engines were supplied by Carmichael of Dundee for £3,700, while a mere £500 sufficed for the rolling stock.

The principal early shareholders were the Dundee council, Messrs. G Kinloch, Wm. Ogilvy the Earl of Airlie and Lord Wharncliffe. Together with D. Ogilvy of Clova, the last two named gentlemen were the principal landowners

Dundee, Ward Road station.

along the line of route. As well as being the earliest venture in Scotland, the company stayed in existence from 1826 to Grouping in 1923, being leased to a succession of other companies, ultimately the Caledonian Railway in 1865, while the line was eventually improved and modernised as the directors raked in rent and dividends. These were certainly not prolific, as large sums were spent in quieting shareholders, compensation and the provision of a accommodation bridges and the like, with the result that funds grew short by 1829 and bitter words were spoken against Landale, a mere 'apothecary' in the view of some. On 29th. May 1830 an Act was obtained for additional funds and for the provision of an extension to the harbour in Dundee. The actual line through Dundee was, in its final form, built without Parliamentary authority and was built by the Trustees of the Harbour Branch Railway. It ran from Ward Road station, along Lindsay street, across Nethergate then east along Yeoman Shore road towards the quay of Earl Grey Dock. The line was constructed subject to stringent restrictions such as a speed limit of 3mph., use of horses only, a limit of two wagons at a loading and no passenger traffic. The line closed in June 1861 when the terminus at Ward Road was finished with.

Out of Ward Road the line first climbed the Law Incline of 760 yd. at 1 in 10 to the first level which ran for 4 miles 1,169 yd. at a more modest 1 in 25. Then followed a stretch of 2 miles 179 yd. and a slight rise of 1 mile 835 yd., then a level 1,007 yd. on to the summit of the line at Hatton, 532ft., from where the incline descended at 1 in 13 to Newtyle, about eleven miles in all. The Law tunnel was 330 yd. in length and the loads on the Law incline were to be of 20-24 tons including the ballast brake wagon of 4 tons. On the incline was a central passing place with a single line of rails below and three rails above it, loads sharing the common centre rail. At Balbeuchly and Hatton the load limits were 16 tons and there were only single lines above and below the passing loops.

The line was opened on 16th. December 1831 following further support from Dundee Council, and up to 1833 traction between the inclines was provided by horses. From September 1833 steam locomotives made their appearance, namely the 'Earl of Airlie' (No .1) and 'Lord Wharncliffe' (No.2) supplied by Carmichael of Dundee. No. 3 'Trotter' was supplied by Stirling of Dundee Foundry in March 1834, while No. 4 'John Bull' was built by Robert Stephenson & Co. and reached the scene in April 1836. Together the four engines were a bargain for those days at £3,300. Nos. 1 and 2 had leading single drivers and a four wheel trailing bogie which immediately made them a 'first' in inaugurating such a device, though colliery engines at Wylam had dabbled in something similar earlier on. Vertical cylinders of 11 x 18in. were provided with 4 ft. 8 in. diameter driving wheels and a total weight of 9 tons 10 cwt. No. 3 was of some distinction as Archibald Sturrock of Great Northern Railway fame had served his apprenticeship on this engine. No. 4 was a four coupled inside cylinder engine. Nos. 1 and 2 were withdrawn in 1854, No. 1 being used as a stationary engine at Errol. 'Trotter' was withdrawn in 1849.

No profits were made and no dividends were ever forthcoming, and by an Act of July 1836 new capital was raised to pay off the Bedlington Iron Company for the rails supplied, as well as placating those who had loaned money.

C.R. No. 15195 on branch train at Alyth.

Chapter 2

The much maligned Charles Landale had, as mentioned, considered other lines of route from Dundee, one easier one to Newtyle, the north east to Forfar, but considered his ultimate choice as the best, envisaging that from Newtyle his line could more easily be extended in both directions east and west. In the 1820s steam traction was not thought to be reliable in the days prior to the Rainhill Trials, so inclined planes were resorted to as a 'safe' means of transport. Landale also wrongly assumed that the flow of traffic each way would be balanced in tonnage, with lime, coal, metalware, manure and flax products for bleaching coming out of Dundee, while grain, potatoes, stone and finished flax would return. In the event more came out of Dundee than went in, having two inclines to face as against the one in the other direction.

Although goods traffic loomed large on the scene, with up to 170 wagons on the books, the company were nevertheless anxious to promote passenger services, offering day tickets, workmen's and season tickets for the labouring classes. As of the period, coaches resembled stage coach bodies on rails with 1st Class outside and Second on top. Given a puffing steam engine, a windy day, the tunnel and three inclindes, if an 'outsider' were wearing his top hat the jaunt could well be an exciting one! The classic anecdote connected with the early days of the line tells of the old countrywoman going to market with her basket of produce and being in progress down one of the inclines when a rope broke, as apparently often did in those days. When they arrived at the bottom with nothing more than a brisk jerk her eggs were found to be

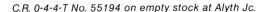

C.R. 0-4-4-T No. 55194 on empty stock at Alyth Jc.

10

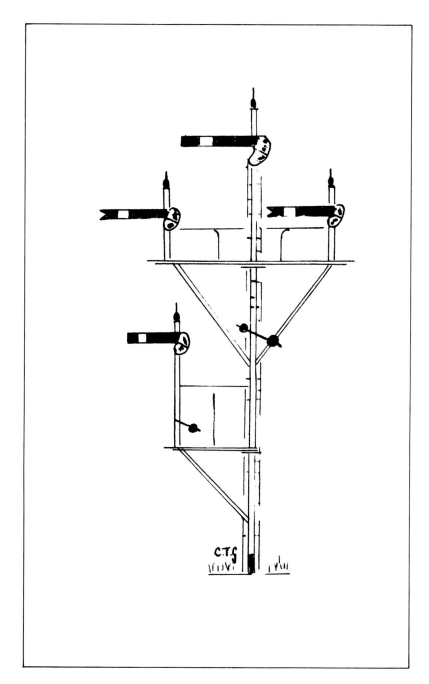

smashed,and her comment on the event was to say that she had really enjoyed the trip but thought that the arrangements were rather on the wild side!

Possibly the peak of passenger traffic in these early days was round about July 1835 when 7,538 folk were carried at 1s.6d. per head inside and 1s. outside. In 1844 the line was earning £700 per mile per year and paradoxically there was no lack of traffic. The trouble stemmed from the involvement of five steam engines for each trip, three of them stationary and two on the levels, plus all the staff involved. The future of the inclined planes was most uncertain.

In October 1844 came a plan to lease the line, which passed under the aegis of the Dundee & Perth Railway by the Act of 27th. July 1846 on the 999 year lease at a rent of £1,400 per annum. The Dundee & Perth line was opened on 24th. May 1847 and the company also took a lease on the Dundee & Arbroath Railway of 19th. May 1836, the name of the combined concern now becoming the Dundee & Perth & Aberdeen Jc. Railway by the Act of 31st. August 1848.

One of the prime faults of the original conception of the Dundee & Newtyle was that there was nowhere to go from the latter place, then a 'green field' site, until in 1832 Lord Wharncliffe built a 15 acre village round the station which rose to a population of 505 ten years later.

As was the intention, short lines were soon laid in, running together to the north of Newtyle for about one mile, then diverging to Coupar Angus (5½m) to the west and Glamis (spelt at times Glammis) (7½m) to the east. Both were of 4ft. 6in. gauge and were constructed by William Blackadder of Glammis. Here horses were used, though it is said that an engine 'Strathmore' was in use on occasion, as well as one of the D & N locomotives. Like many lines at this time, the Coupar Angus line had ideas above its station and a smouldering ambition to extend through Blairgowrie towards Dunkeld.

The two extensions from Newtyle were opened by 4th. June 1838 and a contemporary observer reported the steam engine at work on the Coupar Angus line and certainly to Glamis on 18th. February 1842, though usually the line was worked by horses, with one First and one Second class coach in each train between 1st. July 1842 and 30th. June 1843.

Mr. M'Intosh of Meigle apparently fitted up one of the carriages to work between Coupar Angus and Newtyle by wind power, fixing up a tarpaulin on a stake to the roof of a carriage, while the horse followed in case the wind failed en route. Rather a supernumerary effort for the horse, one would have thought, and putting one in mind of the much later Spurn Head Railway, which also tried wind force. This contrivance was used for four years to 1841, when 'Strathmore' was brought into use, working trains until the advent of the Scottish Midland Junction Railway of 1848.

In 1852 'Wallace' a D & P & A Jc. Railway engine of 1847 was put to work on the Newtyle line and became their No. 8. Its gauge was altered from 5ft. 6in. to the 4ft. 8½in. required. Around 1854 there were three Bury four wheeler engines on the Newtyle line which had been bought secondhand and numbered 10, 11 and 12. They were known as 'Tods' for some reason and had 5ft. wheels.

By the Act of 31st. July 1845 the Scottish Midland Junction would run from Perth to the Arbroath & Forfar Railway at Forfar. Both the small companies, the Newtyle & Glamis and the Newtyle & Coupar Angus were empowered to sell their lines off to the S.M.Jc., and the purchases were completed in January 1846 at a cost of £13,965 for the Coupar Angus line and £16,394 for the Glamis. Both were of course to become part of the new, through east-west line and the Coupar Angus line closed in November 1847 with the curve from Newtyle to Ardler Jc. not reopening for 14 years. The Newtyle-Eassie stretch remained in use until October 1847, after the Eassie-Glamis section had closed some 15 months earlier.

One assumes that the Dundee & Newtyle continued its to-ing and fro-ing, inclines and all while the changes took place in the vale.

As mentioned, the Dundee & Perth leased the Newtyle line, seeing its financial dilemmas, and also the Dundee & Arboath Railway, the whole forming a sizeable line along the north bank of the Tay, save for the hiccup between West and East stations in the Dundee, and given the name of the Dundee & Perth & Aberdeen Jc. Railway.

Here then were rapid railway developments, and now a chance to iron out the deficiencies of the Newtyle line which stood out like a sore thumb. By the Widening, Altering and improving Act of 2nd. July 1847, the gauge was to be altered and the line widened throughout, including the opening out of Law tunnel. The sharp curves at Baldragon and Baldovan, which, it had been

Class 5 No. 45463 brings on Up freight off the Highland section at Stanley Jc.

pointed out, were really only suitable for horse traction, were to be eased, while one of the inclines was to be by-passed by a deviation between Rosemill and Auchterhouse. For a week in early September 1849 the line was closed for the change of gauge, while engines Nos. 1, 2 and 4 were likewise converted. 'Trotter' was scrapped and in 1850 the engines became Nos. 10-12. One can note an early attempt at preservation when, in about 1864, the 'Earl of Airlie' was restored for photographic purposes. (above)

In 1860 two locomotives were built by Stephenson & Co. for the Newtyle line at £1,900 each, becoming Nos. 16 and 17. These were again 0-4-0s and became Nos. 72-3 on the Caledonian Railway. In 1887 one was still at work in the goods yard at Broughty Ferry.

Things were now looking more respectable, though perhaps not proceeding rapidly enough, so that a further improvement Act was sought and granted on 21st. July 1859, which again mentioned the deviation at Auchterhouse and a more impressive one south of Baldovan round to Ninewells Jc. on the Dundee & Perth line. The first was opened on 1st. November 1860 and removed Balbeuchly station from the map, though it created new ones at Dronley and Auchterhouse, the latter one having to be moved on to the new line of route. The second deviation made a dramatic swing westwards and eastwards, opening on 10th. June 1861 and closing the Law incline, tunnel and Ward Road terminus. However, three stations now appeared at Lochee, Victoria and Liff. Victoria was renamed Camperdown on 1st. May 1862 and, again, Lochee West on 1st. February 1896. The station closed on 1st. January 1917.

The fortunes of the D & P & A Jc. Railway changed; in 1863 the line was taken over by the Scottish Central, in which the Dundee & Newtyle was vested from 26th, July 1863. Powers were in the air to by-pass the remaining incline at Newtyle in 1864, but the whole concern was absorbed into the Caledonian Railway in 1865 Subsequent developments were a new line from Newtyle (Old) to Meigle (Alyth Jc.) opened on 3rd. August 1868. The station at the top of the incline, Hatton, closed in October 1865. Washington, near Ardler, Kirkinch and Leason Hill, both on the Glamis line disappeared early on, while Fullerton on the Alyth branch became Meigle in 1876, when the old Meigle became Alyth Jc. on the main line.

The D & N technically survived as a corporate existence until Grouping in 1923. The Newtyle diversion was difficult to complete, due the excavation of a rock cutting.

Newtyle village grew to become some half a dozen streets by 1922, with the original station still in use as a goods depot at the end of a short branch from the north, crossing the main east-west road on the level. As seen the diversion which removed the Hatton incline had been made, and approached the village from the west on its north side with the station lying just east of the road going north to Meigle, on the overbridge. From Newtyle station the single line split into two branches running together for a short distance, both curving north west to cross the Meigle road again, the left hand one continuing to the main line at Ardler Jc. largely along the formation of the old line but avoiding another incline thereon. The second line made a sweep

No. 55217 arrives at Blairgowrie.

Newtyle Old station

north and then across the main line to come down running eastwards into Alyth Jc. station on its north side, quite an unusual and rather spectacular move, probably done to enable trains to reach the junction with a minimum of interference to main line trains; the old Glamis line formation, left unused, ran off quite a way eastwards and joined the formation of the main line in the middle of nowhere. Not that the setting of Alyth Jc. was anything more splendiferous. The layout was reasonably pretentious with solid up and down platforms and buildings plus hotel set on the road bridge where the Meigle road took a right angled bend to cross. On the north side was a bay where the Newtyle line came down, facing east and intended for the Alyth branch or as an exit for local trains to Forfar. The descending Newtyle branch trains could proceed directly on to the Alyth branch but not on to the main line or into Alyth Jc. main station into which they had to reverse. There was a platform to accommodate Newtyly-Alyth through services at the back of the down platform, and a short bay on the up side facing west.

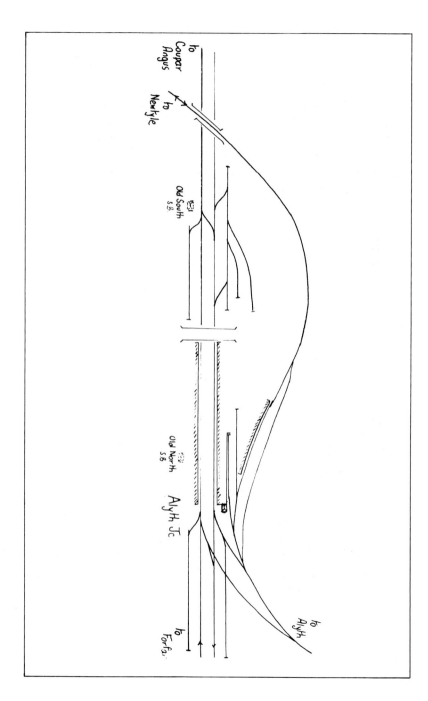

Chapter 3

Looking way ahead: Ardler Jc. closed on 30th. March 1952 so that it was no longer possible to run trains directly from Newtyle to Blairgowrie. Instead they ran to Alyth Jc., where they ran round, the coaches being propelled on to the Alyth branch, then forward wrong line through the station wrong line and back on to the up line for right away. Trains from Alyth terminating at the junction ran into the down line and not the bay, as expected.

For a time the Law tunnel, which ran beneath what was considered to be an extinct volcano, was used by the Scottish Mushroom Company, while the engine house for the incline sought modest fame as a tennis pavilion. From Ninewells Jc. the diversion swung round through Liff and Lochee to Fairmuir Jc., where there was a goods branch to Maryfield Depot. Lochee did well with its jute works, but there was little local passenger traffic as the diversion was time-wasting and the Dundee tramcars were handier. Then came Baldovan & Downfield, where the new line followed the original route to Baldragon and then Rosemill signal box which oversaw a couple of quarries and a manure works. From here the line ran up at 1 in 74 to Auchterhouse station and the summit; thereafter it ran on for two miles of level pegging past Pitnappie Siding, then down a steady 1 in 60 to Alyth Jc. Newtyle station was at 16m.61 ch. from Dundee.

As mentioned, Alyth Jc. was really a railwaymen's station on the Perth-Aberdeen line, being really situated only about one mile south of Meigle, a

4F 0-6-0 No. 44314 enters Coupar Angus from Blairgowrie.

sizeable village on the main road between Coupar Angus and Forfar. The 5¼m branch line to Alyth left Alyth Jc. at the eastern end, then curved north west skirting Meigle on the east side, Meigle has two claims to fame, one as the birthplace of the Liberal Prime Minister, Sir Henry Campbell Bannerman, the other more insubstantial as that of King Arthur's Guinevere. The Alyth Railway was a separate company which opened the line on 12th. August 1861, being transferred the Caledonian Railway in 1875. Meigle station was originally called Fullerton after a nearby house, to make matters a little more complicated. Three and a half miles further on came Jordanstone station, then a mile further Pitrocknie Platform for the local golf course before the line ran into Alyth from the east. Alyth was a small weaving and carpet making township, with a linen works, a wollen mill and a modest cattle market. The station was set neatly to the south of the town and the single line branched into one platform which had a small wooden all-over roof at the buffer end, a three road goods shed and turntable.

Chapter 4

We now turn to the west end of Strathmore and look more closely at Perth, at one time the capital of Scotland, being an excellent centre of communication at a crossing of the Tay end at a place where north-south routes crossed those between east and west. The Council of Perth, local merchants and landowners grew tired of high charges levied for cartage by road and canal and instituted a survey of the Strathmore area with a view to planning railways, though nothing came of this immediately after 1825 when it was

Blairgowrie branch train approaching Coupar Angus.

No. 55217 at Blairgowrie.

carried out. However, with the development of railways in the south of the country the citizens of Perth became interested in linking up with the embryo system, primarily for goods traffic.

The General station at Perth was opened in 1847, with William Tite as architect and Messrs. Locke & Errington as engineers. Interested signatories were representatives of the Scottish Central, Scottish Midland and Edinburgh & Northern Railways. For many years the station was regarded as one of the largest in Britain and something of a gateway to the more spectacular scenery of the Highlands to the north. In 1848 the line was opened to Forfar by the Scottish Midland Jc. Railway, eventually to be taken over by the Caledonian in 1866 as part of their prime route from Carlisle. From the direction of Stirling came the Scottish Central line which of course connected with the S.M.Jc.R. at Perth, while in from Ladybank came the Edinburgh, Perth & Dundee Railway, later called the North British. As originally planned, there were three involved companies at Perth, with the Caledonian regarding the station as a through one on the route from Carlisle to Aberdeen, while the Highland Railway came as far south as Stanley Jc., some 7¼m. to the north and gained Perth by way of running powers. Similarly the North British reached Perth from the south over two miles of running powers from Hilton Jc.

From Perth it was one time possible to radiate in ten directions, with the CR claiming six of these, to Edinburgh, Carlisle, Glasgow, Aberdeen, Crieff and Dundee. The Highland had only one route, and a mammoth 305 miles at that from Wick, but was careful to arrange connections at Perth with all important places. The remaining three routes ran in from the south by way of the NBR, that is, two from Edinburgh via the Forth Bridge and via Ladybank and the line form Glasgow via Alloa and Kinross.

For its size Perth station was remarkably straightforward, with main up and down platforms, the longer being 1,745 ft. and with the main entrance off the Glasgow road. There were a north and south bay line on the west side of the station, and a side platform on the east side, while here also on the east side up and down platforms were set on the Dundee line as it curved away, having the road approach shared with a common entrance and concourse in the 'Y' made by the diverging lines, while to the right was the station hotel built in the best Scottish chateau style.

At a little over 1½ miles north of Perth the Almond Valley & Methven Railway, which was opened on 1st. January 1858 branched off to the west. This was, like many others of the period, an independent railway and became part of the Scottish North Eastern in 1864. Thereafter, in 1865 the line was extended to Crieff, in effect by-passing the town of Methven to the south, so that Methven Jc. was put in, 1¼ miles away and a short branch was laid in to connect. The shuttle passenger service of six runs each way and one late trip on Saturdays was withdrawn in September 1937, with the services over the main line of 18 miles, including of course Methven Jc. going in September 1951. While the Methven branch was open, Methven Jc. did not always feature as a recognised station in the public timetables and, before closure, was a station for which passengers had to notify their intentions either to join or to alight.

C.R. 0-4-4-T No. 55161 at Kirriemuir.

Chapter 5

Into Strathmore the double line ran through Luncarty (4m.) to Strathord (5m.) where the three mile long light railway to Bankfoot left. Again the line was independent, opened on 7th. May 1906 and becoming part of the Caledonian in 1913, truly independent in that it had its own station adjacent to the main line and only accessible to through trains by a back shunt in the sidings. There were six services daily on the branch, and a midday extra on Saturdays, while odd trains were known to run through to and from Perth and, on occasion, to Stanley Jc. Passenger services on the branch were withdrawn on 13th. April 1931, succumbing to the nearby road competition, while goods lingered for a further twenty years or more.

An Aberdeen to Perth local enters Alyth Jc.

At Stanley Jc. the Highland Railway joined for its final run to Perth, eight miles away, where its single track became double each side of the down island platform before joining the Caledonian at the south west end. The signal box was set in the angle of the junction and also supervised goods lines with a warehouse on the up side, while adjacent to it on the down side a facing connection ran, unusually, into a couple of sidings, probably devised to enable traffic off the HR to back in if necessary. Stanley village lay a short way from the station to the south.

The line which had been following the course of the Tay now crossed it west of Cargill village at the point where the river Isla joins, and after leaving

22

Kirriemuir Jc. with ex C.R. 4-4-0 No. 54486 coming off the branch.

Ballachie Goods Siding turned to run due east to Cargill station (11m.) a small affair set at a respectable distance north east of its village with the building on the north side and signal box on the south side controlling a small yard. At 13 miles was Woodside & Burrelton station, serving two villages which both lay south of the line and both close at hand. Also close by was the evocative Strelitz Wood. No doubt competing traffic on the nearby A94 Perth-Brechin road would tend to stifle any local railway passengers, and the line turned north east to run alongside it to Coupar Angus (15½m.). Woodside & Burrelton was renamed Burrelton only from September 1927.

Coupar Angus is another of those many oddities, situated in Perthshire in spite of its name, though there are vague remains of a Cistercian abbey just south of the station site which had most of its estates situated over the boundary in nearby Angus, which may explain things. Here is a small town of about 2,200 containing a preserves factory, tannery, malteries, jute and linen works, also a timber yard and market. The station was of suitable size and attracted stops by the more important trains. Offices were at ground level on the north side with a driveway up from the Railway Hotel, and the platforms were gained by footbridge to a down side island, complete with offices girt about with a verandah, and a single up platform. The outer face of the island dealt with the Blairgowrie branch, which ran West for a short way parallel with the main line over the town's High Street level crossing, before curving north west. There was a fair sized goods yard on the town side of the station, with shed and 6 ton crane, while the south side had sidings to the timber yard at the west end.

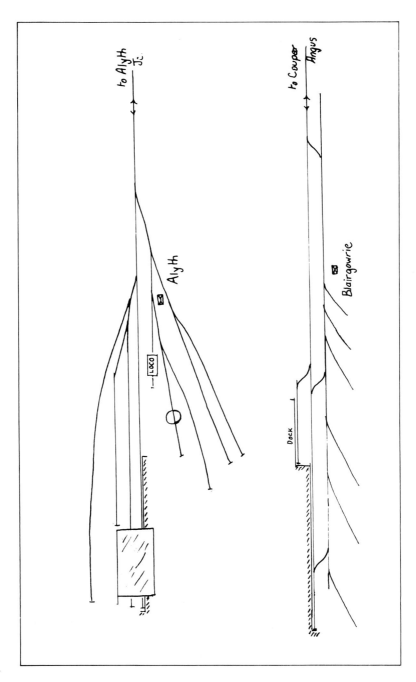

to Alyth Jc.

Alyth

LOCO

to Coupar Angus

Blairgowrie

Dock

The Railway Clearing House Book of Stations gives private sidings for Messrs. Gentle, Panton and Wigglesworth. One signal box worked the crossing and the central section, while there was a smaller cabin at the east end on the north side of the line where the down loop came in.

Blairgowrie, set some five miles to the north of the main line at the point where the Highlands begin, is a singularly unremarkable town for its size, bigger than Coupar Angus at 5,500 and with fruit and linen as its sustaining industries. The river Ericht comes down from the north and divides the town, rather like a small Budapest, from its partner on the other bank, Rattray, which tends to be the solely residential pattern. The railway ran up the bank of the river right to the centre of Blairgowrie at the town centre, and had a covered in platform with the main row of admin. buildings on the side which faced the river. There were three adjacent hotels, so that business here was expected to be good. Nearby the bridge over the river linking the two parts of the town made rail access very convenient and the service of trains numbered ten each way to and from Coupar Angus with some of them running through from Dundee. In the evening there were two extra arrivals, making matters somewhat unbalanced. At just over 1½m. was the conditional request halt of Rosemount, handy for the golf course. From here the train ran on without much distinction to Coupar Angus, apart from a bowstring girder bridge over the Isla which caused its need for repair during the floods of 1947. The line was constructed by the Scottish Midland Jc. and opened in 1855.

Ardler Jc. looking east.

Chapter 6

Ardler, at 19½m. from Perth was a simple roadside station with about five trains stopping daily each way on the main line, plus those on the Blairgowrie services. The signal box was on the north side near the overbridge, the main building on the south side. There were a loading dock, two ton crane and cattle pen on the north side, while the small village lay close by to the north east, its chief attribute being the church. Ardler Jc., some way to the east of the station and village, was the point where the formation of the old Newtyle Railway and the succeeding branch off diverged, carrying the Dundee trains.

We must now run on through Alyth Jc. and beyond, past an historic area which has already been covered, down the main line to Eassie station at 4m. from Alyth Jc. a larger place than Ardler with a fair sized yard and shed, three ton crane plus signal box on the north side of the level crossing with the station on the west side of the road and, again, with the building on the north side. The whole layout was hidden in the depths of the Muir plantation and the nearby hamlet of smithy, post office and three or four houses would fit nicely into a match box. It is at times hard to justify the building of often quite comprehensive stations in areas of little habitation, except perhaps to satisfy the whim of some local landowner.

Eassie has its own story, namely that of the vicar of the nearby church who when in full spate one Sunday realised that his congregation wished to press on with the gathering in of the sheaves of corn during a wet harvest time and enouraged them, to carry on with the good work immediately afterwards, with

No. 54486 enters the branch at Kirriemuir Jc. with the goods.

Class 5 No. 44801 passes Forfar South Jc. on a Down relief.

the result that, a week later, the roof of the church fell in, presumably by Divine intervention.

Onward along the straight and level line for a further two miles to Glamis station, set, like Eassie, in the middle of a forest and crossed by its road at the eastern end, with a minor road passing beneath the line at the west end. The whole of the yard layout and station buildings were on the south side of the line, leaving the signal box on the north side. Glamis village lay to the south, two miles away, while the stately home of the Bowes-Lyon family stands proudly and secluded on its estate between station and village to the east of the road.

The next point of interest on the line was Kirriemuir Jc., a curiosity in the shape of a low platform set in the angle where the branch from Kirriemuir joined in from the north, trailing in towards Forfar. There is something of Methven Jc. about the site, as Kirriemuir Jc. had nothing about it except the signal box and Mother Nature. The station was opened on 1st. August 1858, four years after the opening of the branch line by the Scottish Midland Jc.. Four trains each way halted; this reduced to one service only after 1st. February 1860 and the station was closed on 1st. May 1861, so that through passengers had to change at Forfar. In 1951 there were still good traces of Kirriemuir Jc., with the low up platform in position and the triangular platform on the down side in the fork of the junction.

Kirriemuir, like Blairgowrie, lay a few miles north of the main line along its somewhat sinuous branch line and was a prime weaving township with a

27

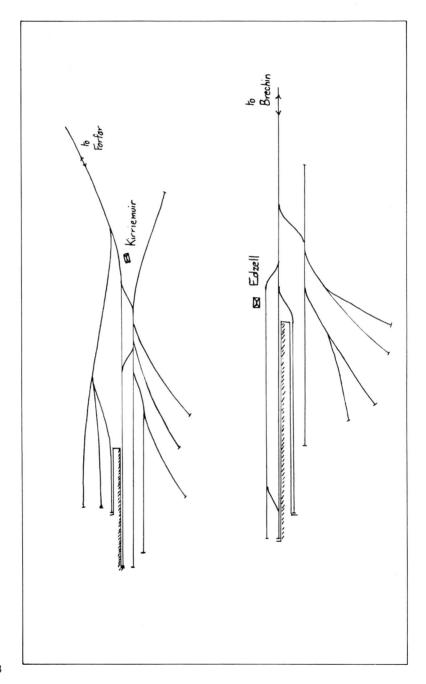

large linen works opposite the station terminus. The line ran in from the east into the town itself and there was a single platform with buildings and an awning. The goods yard and warehouse were on the south side. Not far from here, at No. 9 Brechin road in a five roomed cottage was born Kirriemuir's most famous son, Sir James Barrie. Train services were about 10-12 in number each way and the run was reckoned as between Kirriemuir and Forfar, a distance of six miles, of which half was on the actual branch from Kirriemuir Jc.

After the three miles from Kirriemuir Jc. the outskirts of Forfar were reached, a town of about 10,000 people, noted at one time for the introduction of brogues which were originally fancy shoes made of horse leather, and with such diverse industries as ladder, making, weaving, linen, jute, canning and market gardening. As the line swept into Forfar in a wide arc it met the line from Brechin via Tannadice which joined it at South Jc., coming in in a trailing direction towards the east and running parellel for a short way. The line passed the suburb of Zoar to enter its station on a sharp curve of two platforms with glass verandahs linked by a central footbridge and with the main approach at the south side facing Market street. Therefore the line swung north east as a double tracked spur came up on the right from the old station terminus, serving en route various sidings, a saw mill and the municipal gas works. To the north here the site was filled by a large goods yard and a four road engine shed with turntable. As all this came together at Forfar Jc. a single line was thrown off to the right, being the branch to Dundee East station.

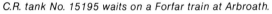
C.R. tank No. 15195 waits on a Forfar train at Arbroath.

Chapter 7

Having arrived at Forfar, roughly in the middle of things, it is time to pause and consider the first of three ways which might be travelled from here; in the first instance, obviously, the line of the old Arbroath & Forfar Railway, for which the seeds had been set by a meeting of the interested landowners and merchants of Arbroath, a town which already numbered some 14,000 in 1841. Again, it was the good folk of Strathmore who needed supplies of line and coal, while also requiring an outlet for produce. Here two wealthy landowners were prominent, the first being the Ogilvies, the second and perhaps more important here, Lindsay Carnegie who was to become Chairman of the A & F until it became part of the Aberdeen Railway in 1848, a man who also became a freeman of Arbroath until his death in 1860.

There was of course the Dundee & Newtyle, but this unremunerative switchback was not regarded as being of much serious worth, though one comment of the period is apposite here:

'Though the shareholders have never received any dividend whatever, yet all the landowners and not a few of the tenants acknowledge that they have been great gainers. Their properties have been increased in value far beyond the money they have sunk in the railway.'

Benefits no doubt accrued to those around Newtyle, but surveys were still made, as by Stevenson, between Brechin and Montrose in the 1820s, later repeated by Grainger and Miller. On neither occasion was anything successful achieved, as Brechin town refused to chip in with half the cost of the survey. Somewhat disgruntled but still anxious for some positive results, a landowner privately paid Grainger and Miller to survey a line from Forfar to Arbroath, a

No. 55193 with stovepipe leaves Forfar for Arbroath.

Kirriemuir goods at Forfar. C.R. 4-4-0 No. 54454.

route which had also been previously covered in 1826 by Stevenson along with Mr. Blackadder of Glamis. Stevenson's idea of an inclined plane into Arbroath was rejected for obvious reasons after the Newtyle experience perhaps, while it was stressed that there should be no lines along public roads to the harbour.

The surveys were approved and an Act was passed at this time of depression before 1840, when Grainger's original estimate of £57,243 for a 15¼ mile single line went up by £11,000, due in part to the rising cost of land and iron used for the rails.

The linen industry had also suffered, so that, indirectly, shareholders became a rarer commodity. Construction went ahead smoothly, apart from some initial wrangling with the turnpike people over the siting of a bridge in the Friockheim area.

The line was opened in January 1839 with the rather odd gauge of 5ft.6in., odd particularly in that it revealed no wish to link up with other lines elsewhere, as in England. Conformity was to arrive when the A & F became part of the through route from Carlisle. Earthworks on the line were light, with the deepest cutting 36ft. and the highest embankment 29ft.

To pre-empt things a little, a service was offered from 28th. November 1838 using a horse drawn carriage the 'Lady Jane' which ran between Arbroath and Leysmill twice daily at a sixpenny fare. However, three engines were ordered from Mr. Stirling's Dundee Foundry Company ready for the public opening, when 565 passengers were carried on the first day. The first engine, originally given the name 'Robert Burns' had this then changed to 'Victoria' (with ships, name-changing is a bad omen), then suffered a mishap on one of its journeys, 'derangement' of bad tubes and poor fuel. Mr. Stirling deducted £10 3s. 11¼d. obviously accurately calculated, and received a bill for £28.2s.6d. incurred by the substitution of horses. Two other engines, 'Caledonian' and 'Britannia' were delivered on 18th. February and 4th. March 1839 respectively and proved essential to the running of things, as did the rolling stock which was ever in short supply. The first year's estimate for passengers carried was 60,000, a figure which was almost reached in half the time. Freight prospered and the transfer to or from rail appears to have been a free-for-all in which tradesman could leave wagons on the line at any point for loading or unloading as they wished, much as the curling excursions elsewhere in Scotland were wont to shed wagons in the early days near the ponds so that the stones might be dropped off. Later additions to the rolling stock were the engines 'Princess' and 'Albert' which no doubt played their part in bringing Forfar or Brechin folk to the sea and Arbroath 'smokies' inland for a breather. For some illogical reason drivers on the line at this period wore white coats and were liable to a fine if these were found to be soiled at the beginning of a new week. Relations with the D & A were friendly and it was possible to work over a line between the two stations in Arbroath and to obtain a through ticket between, say, Dundee and Forfar. By an Act of 3rd. July 1846 a new harbour branch was built in Arbroath, as well as a new station for joint use.

'Crab' No. 42800 at Forfar North Jc. with a lightweight petrol tanker train.

C.R. 4-4-0 No. 54450 on a goods at Forfar North Jc.

During the ten years of free and easy independence which the Arbroath & Forfar enjoyed, services were apparently run on a sort of time interval system without signals or block. This was not absolutely foolproof, as witnessed by the event on 12th. February 1841 when a passenger train and a down ballast train met forcibly outside Clocksbriggs station, headed by 'Victoria' and 'Britannia' respectively, causing quite a destruction of stock and due apparently to the ballast train having left Forfar before time.

Pressures on the A & F by the Scottish Midland Jc. Railway on one side and the Aberdeen Railway from the other towards Guthrie led to the leasing of the line by the latter concern from 1st. February 1848 and its doubling and reduction to standard gauge beginning in September 1846, from which time heavier rails were laid on sleepers instead of the 66,000 or so locally hewn stone blocks hitherto in service. 'Victoria' and 'Caledonian' plus some 1st. Class carriages were also regauged, and the company were somewhat slow in the task, as the D & A., who also suffered the 5ft.6in. gauge had finished their adjustments and found the difference in gauge between the stations in Arbroath inconvenient.

For alterations, the Arbroath-Friockheim section was let to Robert Moffat Jnr. on 30th. July 1846, while the Friockheim-Forfar section went to David Murray. Both sections were to be completed by March 1847, but were not in fact ready until July. A mixed gauge timetable operated from 31st. August 1847, and the broader gauge lasted until October, with the whole line finally converted and finished on 25th. October 1850.

Branches from Brechin and Montrose to Guthrie and Friockheim were completed by the Aberdeen Railway, and the all-round train service was opened on 1st. February 1848. The line had no severe gradients and was well managed, with a high number of passengers. Third Class fares were cheap at not much over ½d. per mile. However, there was some discomfort, as the carriages had no night lighting and little ventilation. Doors were on one side only, and with shutters closed in bad weather daylight was impeded.

Chapter 8

Two and a quarter miles out of Forfar came the little roadside station of Clocksbriggs, scene of the early accident mentioned above. As far as here the countryside is undistinguished and indeed marshy for a time on the south side, while at the station itself there is little to justify its existence except for a large farm called Wemyss and a brace of cottages to go with it. Clocksbriggs was the name, not of a village, but of a big house which lay east of the station on the north side of the line, and which had long vanished by 1923, transferring its name incidentally to the nearby home farm. The station was on the north side of the road underbridge, and there was a small yard on the side as well as a one ton crane.

No. 45355 on a relief Glasgow to Aberdeen express passing Forfar South Jc.

Arbroath to Forfar train at Guthrie Jc. C.R. 0-4-4-T No. 15195.

On now past Rescobie loch on one side and the smaller Balgavies loch on the south side until Auldbar Road station was reached at five miles from Forfar, where there was a small goods yard for all traffic on both sides of the line and a warehouse on the south side. The station building lay at right angles to the layout on the north side of the line adjacent to the road overbridge which was a contrived hump in this flat countryside, carrying a road northwards from the main Forfar-Arbroath highway. Once again there was little hereabouts to generate traffic, and much of this would come from the large village of Letham, some 1 ¾ miles to the south, for which this was the nearest point on the line.

As the line approached Guthrie station the main road and itself ran together, both being closest in the vicinity of the station yard, though the station buildings lay on the north side over the footbridge at the end of the driveway which led up to Guthrie village and castle. At 7 miles from Forfar the station was a much more substantial affair than the others, having an island face on the south side of an up loop line, a down bay platform and goods yard with weighhouse, surprisingly no crane and a turntable. There were signal boxes at each end of the layout, that at the east end controlling the junction from which the main line ran north east towards Montrose and south east to Arbroath. Here was another of those places which were very much railwaymen's stations, as Hellfield on the Midland, where operation is the raison d'etre, rather than local populace.

Chapter 9

The two diverging lines were linked by the so-called Friockheim Fork, a line running north-south so that trains could run between Arbroath and Aberdeen by this route with its northerly junction at Glasterlaw on the Montrose line and its southern end at Friockheim station. The spur was of double track and seems to have been taken up and laid down again at several times in its history, finally departing in 1908, leaving its viaduct as a solid souvenir. Friockheim is the point where the main Forfar-Montrose road joins that from Arbroath, the junction occurring to the west of the village almost beneath the station, which straddled it by a skew overbridge. The station had staggered platforms and a small yard on both sides.

As a German student of long standing, the author was intrigued by the interesting name of Friockheim with its Teutonic overtones, until his curiosity was stilled by Mrs. Daniel of the Angus Folk Museum who kindly unearthed the following notice of 22nd. May 1894:

'The Spinning Mill and Village of Friock, of which Mr. Gardyne of Middleton is the Superior, and Mr. John Andson, Proprietor, holding in Feu, hitherto called 'Friock Feus', from this date henceforward is to be named 'Friockheim' and of which change of designation, this, on the parts of Mr. Gardyne and Mr. Andson, is notice unto all whom it may concern.'

Apparently the 'heim' suffix was introduced at the wish of a number of Flemish weavers who were brought over to Angus by the Andsons, Arbroath, merchants, and settled in Friockheim to develop the flax spinning business at the premises later occupied by Messrs. Douglas Fraser & Sons Ltd.

Forfar to Arbroath train entering Friockheim.

Arbroath to Forfar train passing Guthrie Jc.

At Glasterlaw Jc. where the Friockheim Fork came in, the signal box was on the east side of the junction of double line, and a short way north was Glasterlaw station, at nine miles from Forfar with its building on the west side, a footbridge linking the platforms and, beyond, a small yard on the west side with controlling signal box opposite at the level crossing. Other than East Glasterlaw farm there was nothing of great moment hereabouts.

Over the Pow burn by a short viaduct and the line reached Farnell Road station, three miles further, where there was a neat station in woodland, having its main structure on the south side of its approach running down to the main road, at the other side of which lay the rather isolated police station, for which all the action lay to the north by the underbridge and into Farnell village, near enough for the station to dispense with 'Road' in its title, and possessing school, church, manse, castle and corn mill, though lacking much in the way of cottages. Further out lay Kinnaird Castle and deer park. Again, the station had a simple yard on the village side, with signal box opposite.

At 15½ miles from Forfar came Bridge of Dun station, a different proposition from most of the little roadside premises hitherto dealt with, reminiscent of the watery sites in North Wales such as Afon Wen or Dovey Junction, set near a river mouth in mud flats, in this case the South Esk by Montrose Basin and generally without good road access, though this particular station was in a triangle of roads, one being on a long overbridge at the west end of things, and with a level crossing at the east end when the layout had settled down somewhat. The signal box here governed the final run-in of the branch from

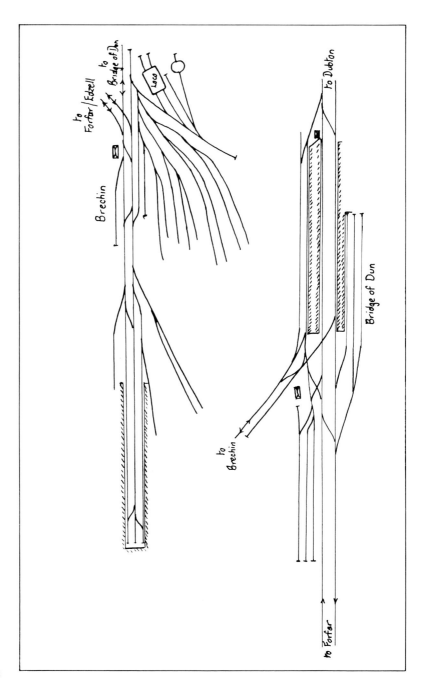

Brechin which had come in from the west and run past the down island platform on its outer face, while to the south were the station buildings overlooking the glass skirted platform structures. The signal box at the west end was substantial, taking in the junction proper and connections to and from the island side, plus three down sidings and a small yard on the down side compete with three tons crane. The actual eponymous bridge crossed the river a few paces to the south of the site, the main line having crossed the water half a mile earlier. Little Dun village and its church lay to the north of the line.

Chapter 10

The branch from here to Brechin was four miles long, and most trains ran through via Bridge of Dun on to Montrose, a total of 9½ miles. The branch line was single to Brechin, where it ran into a terminus just to the east of the town. The station here was of three roads and two side platforms, the centre line being a release for arriving trains, and the building generally was what might be regarded as jolly, displaying lots of glass canopies everywhere both inside and out, nicely neat in arrangement, oblong in shape and with the company name writ large in both cast letters across the front which overlooked St. Ninian's Square; at the present time home for a preserved

Dundee train via Forfar at Brechin.

railway group. Daniels and Dench's 'Passengers no More' has Brechin on the front of the dust jacket, and very attractive too. South of the station proper were a goods yard of respectable size with two five ton cranes, a two road engine shed and turntable, while hard by were two solid looking linen works, Cadhams and the Den Burn. The North British Railway had running powers to Brechin over the route via Broomfield Jc. at Montrose.

Brechin was a little cathedral city of over 7,000, producing whisky, linen and sail cloth, all the more reason to have a branch line which could bring its products down to the sea. The town used to be especially tolerant of beggars, who were all carefully registered and tagged with a pewter badge and allowed to beg freely on Thursdays only until the Poor Law came into force in 1834.

A large signal box here, then, to supervise the station manoeuvres and also the two lines which started off running paralled to each other round the town to the north, the left one continuing after a mile or so as the single line to Forfar, the other veering off due north to form the branch to Edzell.

Originally there was a single line laid in east of the station area running east-north so that trains could work between Edzell and the Bridge of Dun line without reversing in Brechin station. However, this facility had been taken up by 1922.

Down 'Granite City' express at Kinnaber Jc.

The Edzell branch was 6½ miles long and opened in June 1896 with one intermediate station two miles out at Stracathro, originally Inchbare. The country passed through was devoid of great interest and in its heyday the line enjoyed five trains on weekdays only on an out and back basis from Brechin, taking about 20 minutes for the run. The road leading up to Edzell is straight and flat, flanked by pine woods and spanned by the Dalhousie Memorial Arch under which one passes. Then to left and right are, respectively, the Glenesk Hotel and Inglis Memorial Hall, while behind the former, in the intersection of the main road and that to Dunlappie was Edzell station, which thus only impinged on the southern edge of the village. Here was a single platform with its station building and canopy, plus goods yard and two ton crane, as at Stracathro. The village of about 800 folk is laid out rectangularly and shows much more tidiness than is often found elsewhere. Nearby is Edzell Castle with its fine walled garden.

The line lost its passenger service way back, on 27th. April 1931, then reopened on 4th. July 1938, only to close finally on 27th. September 1938, much as the Heanor Gate branch did in Derbyshire.

Chapter 11

From Brechin the Caledonian line round to the north of the station and town back to Forfar 15½ miles away, which it also gained by going 'round the

View from Bridge of Dun looking East.

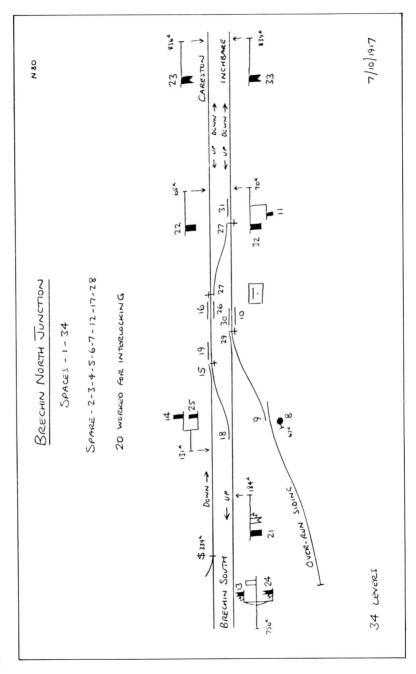

B.I. 61263 at the head of an Arbroath train at Dundee (East) station.

houses' to the north was single line with gentle undulations at 1 in 100 and passing places at the three stations of Careston 5¼ miles, Tannadice 8¾ miles and Justinhaugh 10¾ miles from Brechin. The line was opened to goods on 7th. January 1895 and to passengers on 1st. July 1895, through agricultural territory and was probably laid down with a desire to open up and develop the surroundings. If a station were to be judged by the sort of crane kept in its goods yard, then Careston with a three tonner would be able to pull rank on the other two which could only manage two tons each. The train service was of four or five trains each way on weekdays only and could well have been worked by a Brechin based engine. The service lasted until 4th. August 1952.

As one example of a station site on the line, Justinhaugh most likely took its name from the hotel and bridge over the river South Esk to the north of the line which took in a large sweep round past the Glen Coull distillery at this point. The station had its building and three road goods yard on the south side of things, while the nearby road passed beneath the line.

The third route out of Forfar was that opened by the Forfarshire Railway Company in 1867, nominally independent and running south to Dundee from the North Junction at the east end of Forfar station. The line was single and three were stops at Kingsmuir 2¾ miles, Kirkbuddo 5¾ miles, Monikie 9¾ miles, Kingennie 14¼ miles and Barnhill before Broughty Ferry and Dundee East were reached after 21¼ miles. There were about six trains each way on weekdays only, linked to the branch workings beyond Forfar to Kirriemuir, so that through working between here and Dundee might take some 80 minutes. Services on this line finished on 10th. January 1955.

Kirkbuddo possessed the most powerful crane on the line in its goods yard, a three tonner, though the site was not great, lying to the west of the line along with the station building, the platforms being at the south end. This was a rural setting, with the remains of Kirkbuddo church to the west and, away to the east, Kirkbuddo House with its farmstead.

Chapter 12

The Caledonian main line now ran its last stretch out of Strathmore from Bridge of Dun to Dubton Jc., with the Montrose Basin on its south side. Dubton Jc. was where the line for Montrose set off at the eastern end, to reach the town's Caledonian terminal station (as opposed to the other, North British one) at three miles. From here the main line ran on for a few more miles to reach Kinnaber Jc., where the coast line from Dundee was joined onward to Aberdeen. The station was usually termed Dubton for Hillside, that being the name of the adjacent village to the north. The station layout had a bay on the down side at the west end, while the up side was an island to which the Montrose services could run. The goods yard was also on this side. The station buildings were plainer than at Bridge of Dun, and an approach drive ran up to them on the north side.

After a mile or two the line from Arbroath belonging to the NBR and once the last stretch of the competitive East Coast Route from the south came up from

A Glasgow to Aberdeen excursion passing Dubton Junction.

44

the right hand side at Kinnaber Jc., a cabin made immortal by C. Hamilton Ellis in his book 'The Trains we loved':

'As he pounded up from Montrose, the North British driver saw, far away, the white exhaust of the Caledonian express streaming in the early morning air. The length of the block sections south of Kinnaber favoured the CR and the junction signalman accepted the latter's train less than sixty seconds before he was offered the NB. The East Coast racer was brought to a stand while the West Coast train roared through the junction ahead of it.'

The West Coast trains had a longer run of 539¾ miles with banks at Shap and Beattock, as opposed to the shorter East Coast run of 523½ miles. Up to June in 1895 the East Coast had covered the ground in 11 hours 35 min., culminating in the joint GN., NE. and NB record of 8 hours 40 min. with a light train on 22nd. August 1895. Those were the days, indeed.

A Glasgow relief express approaches Dubton Jc.

Chapter 13

After a chequered start in life, it is pleasant to note that the main line through Strathmore became a fast and efficient route in the 1890s, once the original timber bridges over often unpredictable mountain streams had been replaced, following the sad experience of the Tay Bridge disaster. The long, low structure over the Isla near Coupar Angus on the Blairgowrie branch is a case in point. The 'Dunalastair' 4-4-0s soon got to grips with the first British 60mph. start to stop timings between Perth and Forfar. The branches were busy too, with the little Caledonian tank engines fussing up and down to and from that same main line all the week, never, however, on Sunday, up to the Great War. By the end of the second bout of hostilities the number had already been halved, until some ludricous situations arose, as below when,

No. 72008 'Clan McLeod' enters Coupar Angus with the Up 'Bon Accord'.

to take the Kirriemuir branch as an example, in 1914 there were departures from the little terminus at:

7.30am., 9.45, 10.50, 11.50 (Tues & Fris), 1.10pm., 1.50, 3.50, 5.08 (Tues & Fris), 6.22, 7.05, 8.25 (Sats).
-and a corresponding number on the return journey.

By 1951 the following applied:

| Kirriemuir | dep: 7.22a.m. | Forfar | dep: 5.18p.m. |
| Forfar | arr: 7.34 | Kirriemuir | arr: 5.29 |

The morning train ran all the week, while the evening return was a Saturdays only working, so that there was little point in investing in a day return, or indeed in setting off at all, except on Saturday! Such was the way in which lack of usage could be claimed and closure won.

By the end of 1955 all the branch traffic had gone. One little 0-4-4-T made his mark, however, in 1948 on Glasgow Fair Saturday at Ardler Jc., one mile east of Ardler station, when the 4.20pm. Dundee West-Blairgowrie local overran signals and No. 55180 was struck by 'Jubilee' 4-6-0 No. 45716 'Swiftsure' heading the 3.30pm. mail from Aberdeen. By one of those pieces of good fortune the derailed 'Jubilee' slewed round across the formation and cut the signal wire of the down distant, enabling a down relief train whose crew were vigilant to stop in time as they were approaching at speed. The junction was relaid, but in March 1952 the connections were removed and Ardler Jc. was closed. This caused operating problems at Alyth Jc. for Dundee to Blairgowrie trains until they ceased to run, as these now ran from

Newtyle into the down through branch platform where the engine then ran round and propelled on to the Alyth branch single line, then forward wrong line through the station westwards and then propelled again into the correct position at the up line platform. All in all, with the extra time added to the journey and the tedium of the shuffling to all but the railway enthusiast, this was not an encouragement to passengers to use the through service. Here is the offering for 1951:

Dundee West	dep:	11.28am (SO)	1.12 (SO)	4.20pm	5.40pm	6.55 (SO)
Newtyle	dep:	12.13pm	2.02	5.06	6.19	7.36
Blairgowrie	arr:	12.37	2.26	5.30	6.29*	7.59

* to Coupar Angus only.

Blairgowrie	dep:	7.30am	9.25am	1.15pm (SO)	2.40 (SO)	6.20pm
Newtyle	dep:	7.52	9.59	1.37	3.02	6.45
Dundee West	arr:	8.34	10.36	2.21	3.38	7.20

In 1914, departures from Blairgowrie were as follows:
6.10am, 7.40, 9.00, 10.25, 12.35pm., 3.0, 3.30 (SO), 3.40 (SO), 4.37 (SO), 5.50.

By 1951 the Forfar-Brechin service was also very sketchy:

Forfar	dep:	8.05am	5.23pm		Brechin	dep:	7.0am	2.05pm	6.12
Brechin	arr:	8.31	5.49		Forfar	arr:	7.29	2.30	6.41

Only the 8.05am stopped at Careston, while the 2.05pm only stopped at Justinhaugh in the return direction. From Brechin there were trains out to

CR 0-4-4T No. 55194 on Alyth train at Newtyle

Montrose at 8.30am, 10.20, 1.58pm. and 4.20 (SO)., with arrivals at 7.47am, 10.56, 2.39pm, 4.43 and 6.54, with an odd Saturdays excepted running in from Dubton at 8.07pm.

The Brechin-Edzell branch had finished in 1938, so that the 1914 service is reproduced here to show what was at one time on offer:

Brechin	dep:	7.35am	8.25	11.40 (SX)	12.20 (SO)	3.00	6.02
Edzell	arr:	7.53	8.46	12.09	12.49	3.18	6.20
Edzell	dep:	8.00am	9.15	1.10pm	5.40	6.35	
Brechin	arr:	8.20	9.40	1.29	5.59	7.02	

All trains halted at the intermediate station of Stracathro.

On the Forfar-Dundee East line in 1951 trains left Forfar at 7.43am, 1.00pm (SO), 2.55 (SO) and 6.50, with return workings at 9.20am, 1.08 pm (SO), 4.23 (SO) and 5.50.

Rolling stock was of a remarkably high standard, with two coach sets which were made up into threes or fours as necessary, using either early LMS vehicles or the later ex Caledonian ones. As in several areas in this country, the branch lines never lingered long enough to experiment with the new diesel units which made their debut in West Yorkshire during 1953.

Chapter 14

The main line through Strathmore was, however, to enjoy an Indian summer of high speed running, with fast three hour Glasgow-Aberdeen expresses, to which came the LNER A4s which had been eased out of thier supremacy in the south by diesels elsewhere. On 13th. September 1966 the last A4 No. 60024 'Kingfisher' worked the 17.15 Aberdeen-Glasgow and the 08.25 return the next day, and with the commencement of the winter timetable of 1967 came the sad news of rationalisation whereby all traffic would be routed by way of Dundee and Arbroath. From 3rd. April 1967 all through freight, except for one sole Fife-Aberdeen mineral working and the return empties was withdrawn from the Strathmore line and transferred. On Sunday 3rd. September 1967 the last train from Glasgow passed eastwards at 17.10, with the last service from Aberdeen leaving at 17.30, both passing near Coupar Angus. The ultimate working was the 18.35 Aberdeen-Perth milk and parcels. The reader is referred to John Thomas's 'Forgotten Railways in Scotland' (David & Charles) for more useful information here.

For a time a single line was left in situ to serve Forfar, running from Stanley Jc. for freight only with a 30mph. limit. This has now vanished, and at the time of writing little remains apart from a battered signal box shell at Coupar Angus. The Kinnaber'Jc.-Bridge of Dun section was retained as a single line, running on to the branch for Brechin station which still exists on a tenuous basis, an island of atmosphere as a preservation site housing old rolling stock and relics.

Chapter 15

Mr. G.H. Robin, who kindly supplied the illustrations for this work, also had the forethoght to write down his exploits on the lines in the Strathmore area during the summer of 1948, some of which are recorded here verbatim.

'Sharp at 12.20p.m. we departed with about four passengers and many mail bags from Montrose en route to Brechin. Once again round to Broomfield Jc., but this time we kept straight on past the western face of the disused platform, then under the LNER on our curved way up to Dubton Jc. We did a lot of mail work here, set down the few main line passengers, and on leaving we picked up a wagon for Brechin. As it was marshalled at the rear, and we could not be shunted into the siding, we drew forward and the wagon was manhandled on to us. This process cost us an extra six or seven minutes. Once away we attained only about 43mph. on the easy stretch to Bridge of Dun, where I nipped out and got a single to Brechin (11d). I managed back in time to get shunted about like a chunk of cattle. Evidently the wagon from Montrose was for here, so we had to dispose of the one picked up at Dubton, shunt the one for here and pick up the Brechin one, but this time the loco. did all the heavy work. The 10am. ex Buchanan Street arrived on time with the usual mixed livery and two locos. and required the usual double stop. We were then shunted over the crossover and direct into the outer face of the down island platform.

We left a few minutes late, and an easy run took us into the very cramped terminus at Brechin. I may have used the word 'cramped', but while the space looks somewhat restricted, it is fine and open, and many, many times too ample for today's traffic and appeared to me to be well laid out. We arrived a few minutes after one o'clock at the 'Dubton' platform and found the 2.02pm. for Dundee via Careston and Forfar already standing in the other main line platform and was once more a 'Jumbo' No. 17441 at the head of a two coach set. Had the Edzell branch been open I could have managed it in the time I had; however, I hi-ed off to an hotel and got a good lunch and was back about 1.40pm. I managed a photo. of the station and got a good look at the layout.

The ticket problem cropped up once again, and I decided here to purchase a single for Forfar (3/3d) and to travel on to Dundee with my original ticket as it was no doubt valid for part of the length between Bridge of Dun and Forfar or Dundee. Anyway, it was definitely valid from Broughty Ferry to Dundee East.

The Dobton train left at 1.58pm. almost empty, the signals being cleared for our train almost simultaneously. Quite a few passengers had boarded our train here it left with me in an empty compartment for what proved to be the tit-bit of the 'tour'. We left the platform and like a shot out of a gun charged the junction with a 'wumph' that nearly sent me straight on for Dubton. The Edzell line branched with us and ran parallel for about a mile on a very sharp curve and, I believe, on an up grade of 1 in 50. In due course the branches parted, the Edzell one doing some wild reverse curves before being lost in cutting, while we mounted on at 1 in 100, which bank we topped at 39mph. and speed rose to 50 down the subsequent 1 in 100.

The line, situated in a pleasant and somewhat similar Strath as the main line which ran roughly parallel to us, seemed to have only three grades: ie. up or down 1 in 100 and level. The five and a quarter miles to Careston, undulating but mostly up took us 9 min. 18 secs. Of course, I thought we would have been days early, but got rather a surprise when, on referring to the timetable found that we were allowed 9 minutes to leave! Our 9+ minutes meant that we had averaged 33.8mph. start to stop.

The station, which was in wide, open country of the agricultural and pastoral type, with no visible township or hamlet within miles, consisted of two platforms, a passing loop fully signalled and a very clean and tidy appearance and was devoid of passengers, though having a little parcels traffic.

On leaving, after a 12 second stop we fairly stormed again, this time up to 53mph. on a down grade of 1 in 100, after which we shut off and coasted the next undulating stretch to Tannadice, speed falling and rising according to grade, and we took 5 min. 50 seconds for the 3½ mile section, allowing six minutes to leave.

This proved to be another isolated outpost, but had only one platform and no passenger traffic. We left in 17 min. 14 sec. from Brechin-45 seconds late.

It was now down to Justinhaugh, with nothing special to report and we took 3 min. 25 sec. start to stop for the two miles, which was our shortest station to station stretch. This station, consisting of two platforms and a passing place, is on the southern fringe of the township from which it gets its name, and mile post '4' adorns the eastbound platform. Like the other stations on this line it is smart and well kept. There was a little passenger traffic here and we left in 19 min. 35 sec. from Brechin, being now 25 sec. on the right side of time. Right from the end of Justinhaugh platform we were on another up of 1 in 100 and made the surrounding countryside echo with our exhaust to attain 37¼ mph on about one mile of rising.

This was followed by a somewhat easy descent to Forfar South Jc. with a maximum of 47½ mph, though we coasted for quite a fair length and speed gradually dropped as we approached the main line. On reaching the home signal we reduced speed drastically for tablet exchange and then we coasted again for about half the length hence to Forfar, but opened up again sufficiently to enable us to draw up in Forfar's down main platform dead on time in the prescribed 28 min. from Brechin. After discharging our passengers we drew forward and backed in to the bay platform, where a couple of mechanics did some repair work to No. 17441. It looked to me to be the springs of the driving wheels, and the crews were changed.

To conclude this bit I must say that this is the tightest timing (scheduled) I have yet experienced, and only approaching Tannadice and in the region of Forfar South Jc. could a few seconds have been economised and certainly not more than a minute.

We left Forfar five minutes late and took the right fork at the North Jc. and entered a deep cutting, which I had noticed before but had put it down as part of the yard. As at Brechin, the track immediately seemed to curve right round the town in question. At long last we stopped turning and came out on to a straight stretch. This bit was downhill at first, but changed into a long straight rise at 1 in 70 or 80 into a cutting and through a bridge at the top, where Kingsmuir platform is located. The weather had been fairly bright on the previous section with a very strong south-westerly wind, but now it was much

colder and the wind a nuisance, and this, coupled with the poor efforts of the engine-you'd scarcely think it was still 17441-did not encourage even me to open the windows except when I wanted to see something special.

I took a few times and speeds, but the countryside was fairly featureless except for a few brief glimpses of the Tay estuary as we wound down the hillside at what appeared to be an angle of 45 degrees to the coastline.

Upon leaving Barnhill in a rock cutting we turned sharply westward and crossed the Dundee & Arbroath Joint line on a flyover and joined the main line at Broughty Ferry. Unfortunately a man came in here to keep me company, and I missed the opportunity to take in the approach from Camperdown Jc. to Dundee East, at which junction we were momentarily stopped for signals. PW men were in the act of relaying opposite the signal box, and they probably caused our halt, following which we nosed right across the station to the northernmost platform where we arrived 7¼ min. late, after a very insipid run. Still, it was another section, and a hilly one at that which I could write off.

As I had only 40 minutes to squander, and the satisfying effect of my Brechin lunch was now fading fast, I went in search of a snack meal, but met with no success and as I did not have time to partake of a proper meal, I wasted no time and made for the West station. Here I got a single for Alyth (4/2d.) and found the train in the rear of Platform 2. Once again it was two coaches and in front was a 5P in charge of three corridors-the 4pm. for Brechin-just about to leave. I spotted the refreshment room and popped in and got a savoury and a couple of very pleasant and appetising sandwiches and, being outwith 'the hours' a bottle of lemonade. I nipped out smartly and booked an empty in the 4.20 which took on a good sprinkling of passengers. About this time, and to my disappointment, 0-4-4T No. 15198 backed on frontwards, complete with stovepipe lum which put paid to any chance of my getting a photo. as I refuse to waste any exposures on such atrocities, and I heard the guard say that we'd probably go by Ayth Jc. as the Newtyle-Ardler Jc. line had been closed in the morning. (It was still closed the next Friday 23/7/48 and was being used by a ballast train on Sunday 1/8.)

The weather was quite dull when we left here one minute early and I just noted station times, as I was principally interested now in the historical aspects of this section, over which I had already travelled in the reverse direction. At Liff we had the strange experience, to me at any rate, of picking up a pilotman who carried the tablet. He appeared to be of clerical grade, and wore a smart lounge suit and armband, and we dumped him and his tablet at Lochee. Nothing happened which was exciting until after Auchterhouse, when we tore down the hill and speed rose to an uncomfortable 45mph. as we jerked alarmingly round the spiral curves, but this was toned down to 40 before sliding gently into Newtyle. There was no sign of the Alyth train, and I was told, but only upon asking, that I did not require to change for Alyth Jc. This confusion was because of the Ardler Jc. accident two days before.

Here the sun shone brightly, and I begrudged the time we sat here with 15198 and her stove pipe, as I particularly wanted a photo of this station. Leaving again one minute early we went easily down over the main line and into the through branch platform at Alyth Jc., arriving one minute early. Here I alighted and No. 15195 which had been lying on the passing loop with two coaches, propelled into the Newtyle section and followed the Blairgowrie train as she vacated the through branch platform for the down main for reversing purposes.

If my memory now serves me correctly, I was the only passenger in the branch train for Alyth, when a typically 'due for retirement looking, and overweighted lump of a driver opened the throttle about five minutes late and took us on our uninteresting meander past Meigle and Jordanstone and into the covered terminus at the end of a short branch. There was very little to report here: featureless countryside, gathering rain clouds, a sleepy little platform on the west side at Meigle, just stopping short of the main road level crossing. This is the Perth-Forfar main road and I had passed this spot often. Jordanstone seemed to be just a glorified halt.

As it was as good as raining at Alyth, I toyed with the idea of getting by hook or by crook to Kirrie, and so do that branch also. However, there was not a suitable bus, and I did not wish to hire, and the risk of thumbing was out of the question of time, and also there was the prospect of delay on the main line in the region of Ardler Jc. and a prospect of late arrival in Glasgow.

Returning, there were about nine or ten passengers for the main line, but about a mile or so outside Alyth we stopped at very small and overgrown halt in a cutting and hidden behind a road bridge, and dropped two passengers who took to the fields. At Meigle we halted with the engine on the aforementioned level crossing, to the disgust of road users. It was now only a mile or two to the junction where we entered directly into the down main platform. The throng immediately crossed over to the up platform, but I had a wee scout round. The station proved to have a most interesting layout, not to say peculiar. I had often wondered why the array of four tall signals on the up entrance to the branch platform.

15195 did some shunting and I went on to the road bridge which crosses the west end of the station and which afforded a fine study. However, the rain came down in sheets and I was forced to shelter in the doorway of a most convenient hotel, and finally 15195, who had rounded the train, set off with her two empties in the direction of Forfar, leaving all quiet. I thought I might just manage to get my tea in this hotel, but on enquiry was told it was not yet ready, and as I had only 20 min. I could not risk waiting. I returned to the station and studied the layout further and a down goods passed headed by a 5P, checked through the station by signals. I was returning to the bridge when suddenly I heard a shrill whistle in the distance and a compound exhaust filled the air as it moved a train from standstill. At first I was puzzled, but on consulting the timetable I discovered it was the 5.20pm. from Dundee to Blairgowrie, diverted, leaving Newtyle, and I got a fine view of her coming down into the junction. It would be fine now, but my Scottish pride would not let me photograph a compound on such undisputedly Caley territory. After rounding her train with about six passengers, No. 1123 was halted in the down main and the up home signal went clear. In a few minutes while the Blairgowrie train was held, my train came in with No. 5774 at the head of four passenger corridors and six or seven luggage vans. I got an empty and 1123 crossed over with her train in front of us and right away. No. 5774 came off and I thought that perhaps they were going to combine us to Coupar Angus; however, I asked a porter and found that 5774 was picking up a van somewhere beyond the bridge. As it was now pouring again I could not see much but was prepared for a long wait until 1123 got clear of the scene of Saturday's smash. I realised now that I could have got my tea, bed and breakfast as well in the hotel.

At about 6.40pm. roughly ten minutes late we pulled out and now I looked forward, with all due respect to the seriousness of the situation, to having my first close-up of a railway smash. We were not long in coming to it and got a long drag through the area concerned. The last coach of the local was sitting on her wheels on the branch line, and a heavy wooden beam was being used as a brake across the rails. It was a Caley six wheeled bogie composite and had the offside (in its direction of running) panels torn off, and as it was the corridor side, it left the compartments open to view. Apart from this, it was practically undamaged and must almost have missed being involved. This was followed by some odd wreckage, then an ordinary LMS 3rd. Class corridor bogie was stretched, right way up, half on railway territory and half in a field. Next was the wreckage of the mail vans. What a blessing that they had been devoid of human cargo! They were splintered and telescoped, and had forced their way into the wet earth in the field or had wedged themselves tightly into the bed of a fairly broad ditch. I saw no trace of the local engine, so hurried across the compartment only to find that the express engine had also been removed. The double track had been relaid, but the junction was not laid in. It will be of interest to note that I looked for the locos. at Forfar, Perth and Stirling, but found no trace'.

Some closure dates for stations and lines in the area.

Edzell-Brechin	27th. September 1938 (originally closed 27th. April 1931 and reopened 4th. July 1938)
Alyth Town-Alyth Jc.	2nd. July 1951
Kirrieumuir-Forfar. (Kirriemuir Jc.)	4th. August 1952
Blairgowrie-Coupar Angus	10th. January 1955
Alyth Jc.-Dundee West.	10th. January 1955
Forfar North Jc.-Broughty Ferry	10th. January 1955
Cargill, Stanley Jc., Burrelton, Eassie, Glamis	11th. June 1956
Glasterlaw	2nd. April 1951
Dubton	4th. August 1952
Forfar-Kinnaber Jc.-Stanley Jc.	4th. September 1967

The Angus Railway Group has produced three Steam Albums which contain some very interesting and relevant photographs of stations in both Perth and the Angus areas. These are recommended to readers, and the following dates are taken from the booklets in question with due acknowledgement:

23rd. March 1872	Engine boiler exploded at Bridge of Dun, causing severe injuries to crew.
1st. June 1896	Brechin-Edzell branch opened.
2nd. November 1898	Runaway cattle train ran into the terminal buffers at Brechin, causing much damage to station building and killing many beasts.
20th. October 1899	Collision between passenger and goods trains at Coupar Angus. One driver killed.
27th. November 1908	Fire in connection with a passenger and goods train collision at Guthrie.
1912	Inchbare station renamed Stracathro.
1st. January 1917	Lochee West station closed.
28th. October 1940	Pitcrocknie Platform renamed Pitcrocknie Siding.
1st. October 1905	Woodside becomes Woodside & Burrelton
1st. September 1929	Woodside & Burrelton becomes Burrelton.
3rd. January 1942	Loco. sheds at Alyth and Blairgowrie closed.
8th. August 1946	Bus hit by train at Balmuckety Crossing, Kirriemuir. Ten bus passengers killed.
17th. March 1958	Brechin-Careston closed completely.
5th. May 1958	Auchterhouse-Newtyle closed completely.
8th. December 1958	Forfar-Kingsmuir closed completely.
12. 1959	Stracathro closed entirely.
10/1960	Tannadice closed entirely.
28th. March 1964	Auchterhouse-Fairmuir Jc. closed completely.
7th. September 1964	Edzell branch closed entirely.
1st. March 1965	Alyth branch closed entirely.

21st. June 1965	Kirriemuir branch closed completely.
12/1965	Blairgowrie branch closed entirely.
4th. September 1967	Forfar-Justinhaugh closed completely.
18th. December 1967	Ninewells Jc.-Maryfield closed completely.
4th. May 1981	Brechin branch closed completely.
5th. June 1982	Strathmore line closed completely.

Shed allocation to Forfar (63c) in 1950.

4-4-0 54450/4/86.   0-6-0 57324/68/57441. 2-6-0 42738 42800/1.
0-4-4T 55136/61/62/69/72/85/93-5. 55200/14/30.
-and to Brechin: 0-4-4T 55172/85. 55200/14.